Making mathematics pheno

Dave Pratt

Making mathematics phenomenal

Dave Pratt

Professor of Mathematics Education

Based on an Inaugural Professorial Lecture delivered at the Institute of Education, University of London, on 14 March 2012

Institute of Education, University of London
Professorial Lecture Series

**Leading education
and social research**
Institute of Education
University of London

First published in 2012 by the Institute of Education, University of London,
20 Bedford Way, London WC1H 0AL
www.ioe.ac.uk/publications

ｌ⊂◯663434

British Library Cataloguing in Publication Data:
A catalogue record for this publication is available from the British Library

ISBN 978 0 85473 921 9

The opinions expressed in this publication are those of
the author and do not necessarily reflect the views of
the Institute of Education, University of London.

Typeset by Quadrant Infotech (India) Pvt Ltd
Printed by ImageData Group

Biography

Dave Pratt has researched and written extensively on the relationship between technological design and mathematical thinking with a particular focus on probabilistic thinking. Using a design research methodology, he has developed a number of microworlds to support research and learning in knowledge domains such as probability, mechanics and geometry. Prior to his current post, Dave directed the Centre for New Technologies Research in Education at the University of Warwick. His tutoring is now mostly at masters and doctoral level. Dave started his career as a secondary school teacher over a period of about fifteen years, after which he spent many years supporting the initial development of secondary mathematics teachers.

Making Mathematics Phenomenal

Two meanings of phenomenal

Whatever meaning the reader might attach to the word 'phenomenal', it seems that in the broad public perception, mathematics is far from *phenomenal*. A quick look at *Yahoo Answers* (responding to the question, 'Why is maths boring?') reinforces the idea that, far from being 'outstanding', as in one usage of the word 'phenomenal', mathematics is perceived as boring:

> *Respondent X: You may not feel like it leads to anything. It's a bit pointless really, but proves your [sic] clever so get a good grade. It's boring because you can't see how it is helping you in later life.*

A second response in *Yahoo Answers* suggests that some people are hard-wired for mathematical thinking and others are not:

> *Respondent Y: It's not you have to know how to understand it and all its intricacies, but even some simple bits like the Fibonacci sequences can be fascinating. Just depends how your mind works.*

I am aware that appealing to *Yahoo Answers* is somewhat unconventional as a research methodology, but there is no shortage of anecdotal and seriously rigorous research to support the notion that those of us who find mathematics outstanding are the oddities because generally mathematics 'is perceived as "hard", "boring" and "useless"' (p. 2) (Osborne *et al.*, 1997, in a report on attitudes for 16-year-olds towards future participation in mathematics, quoted in Brown *et al.*, 2008).

These statements are not surprising to those of us who have worked in mathematics education for many years, but they remind us that we have not yet realised our aspiration that mathematics be seen by the many rather than the few as an extraordinary, indeed 'phenomenal', discipline.

Despite being perceived as pointless, mathematics also carries with it a perceived high level of prestige, perhaps among the most impressive achievements of the human mind. Respondent Y above claimed that mathematics is only for those whose minds work in a particular way; indeed, mathematics is often described as abstract and perhaps this relates to the disconnection with reality that renders the subject pointless, according to Respondent X.

This perception of mathematics as abstract is not a recent development. In Plato's Theory of Forms, the highest and most fundamental kind of reality lies in non-material ideas, and perceived reality is merely a shadow of those concepts. Certainly, pure mathematicians might see the power of their subject in the decontextualized axioms and theorems that rely on logic and not in any requirement that the mathematics speaks directly to the material world; fortunately, it often does, but this is typically portrayed as happenstance rather than the object of the enterprise.

From this point of view, mathematics is not perceived through the senses but lies in an abstract world, which could never really aspire to being accessible to the many. Accordingly, mathematics is in fact the antithesis of phenomenal, not *experienced* out there, but an internal cerebral activity. My argument will seek to justify and exemplify a different view, one that emerges less from the discipline of mathematics and more from pedagogic and philosophical considerations. I will argue that, to be accessible to the many, the teaching of mathematics needs to present the subject not only as cerebral but also as perceived through sensation, like any other phenomenon, and that this is one of the ways in which the many and not just the few will engage with the discipline.

My position is fundamentally shaped by two related influences, one pedagogic and the other philosophical. First, when thinking about teaching and learning, Harel and Papert (1991) have proposed a Constructionist approach, which places emphasis on student ownership that gives them control over their own learning. After decades of developing new visions of schooling based around student-centred use of Logo programming, Harel and Papert argued that the making of artefacts, such as Logo-based projects that are publicly shared, offers an especially powerful context for mathematising. In fact, Logo provided a paradigmatic case of how it might be possible to make mathematics phenomenal, as became clear to me, when, as a teacher, I used Logo with students and witnessed their natural and committed engagement with the power of algebra to communicate with a machine that could create wonderful pictures and animations for them.

Second, when reflecting on the relationship between the mind and the world out there, I am influenced by recent philosophical developments on inferentialism (Brandom, 2002). Inferentialism contests the notion that initial awareness of a concept is grasped solely by reference to its representation. Rather, initial engagement takes place within a web of reasons through which purposes and significances can be inferred. Representations are situated within that inferential structure through the giving and taking of reasons. In applying the inferential argument to education, connections with Constructionism become apparent. Constructionism recognises the primary importance of the giving and taking of reasons by placing the student at the centre of the learning process. The role of the computer in the Constructionist vision is as a machine whose power can be released through mathematical communication, reason enough perhaps to invest in using and learning (mathematical) representations.

Making mathematics phenomenal is a design challenge that embraces both meanings of phenomenal: if mathematics is seen as extraordinary in its power to explain and 'get stuff done', students might engage more readily with its key ideas; and the argument below proposes that such an aspiration might be facilitated by creating an experiential version of those ideas.

To begin the argument, I need to review the notion of mathematical abstraction beyond Plato to its current articulation in the mathematics education literature.

What is mathematical abstraction?

In attempting to explore the nature of mathematical abstraction, the key question that emerges above is the extent to which abstraction depends on decontextualisation, the absence of a material presence. If mathematical abstraction is the hallmark of mathematics and mathematics is seen as purely cerebral, not experienced through the world out there, then it is reasonable to deduce that mathematical abstraction requires a removal from the material world. Certainly, an inspection of the pure mathematics presented in textbooks and university courses reveals little or no reference to contexts and situations (other than in self-evidently contrived ways) and so easily suggests that, if mathematical abstraction is the achievement we see in those textbooks, it is surely decontextualised. Whereas mathematicians may see their ultimate achievement as the creation of formal expressions of mathematics, however, teachers and mathematics educationalists might look elsewhere; their focus is on learning and they may wish to understand more about the process that leads to that achievement. Is the abstraction that takes place in learning mathematics simply a question of getting rid of the context or is there rather some sort of blurring of contexts that takes place?

Many researchers have portrayed abstraction as a strictly hierarchical process, progressing through a series of stages. Dubinksi (1991), for example, proposes that repeatable actions are internalised to form processes, before being transformed into mathematical objects. Sfard (1991) also views the reification of processes into mathematical objects as being the key achievement of abstraction, and later (1994) describes reification as the birth of a metaphor. Gray and Tall (1994) also describe abstraction in terms of processes and concepts, though they see the potential for achievement in the flexibility and freedom to think in terms of either processes or concepts (what they refer to as 'proceptual thinking') and they point to the parallel ambiguity in mathematics itself. For them, the mathematical symbol plays a key role in facilitating this flexibility, so, for example, the proceptual thinker can regard 3 + 5 either as the process of adding 5 to 3 or as the concept, 8. Although these theories present different stories about mathematical abstraction, they share a common belief that there is an ascension to a decontextualised achievement, whether it be a reified object or a procept.

This deep idea has been critiqued, for example by Confrey and Costa (1996), since it remains unclear how the various states of abstraction are achieved. Plato's Forms seem to haunt these process–object accounts of mathematical abstraction. This view of abstraction furnishes a danger that the teaching of mathematics will be hampered by a sense that the mathematics is elusive, only accessible to proceptual minds or to those who are able to reify. These accounts of mathematical abstraction describe the nature of *high-level* thinking (and here I intentionally emphasise the hierarchy) in the organism. In contrast, teachers of mathematics are focused at a micro-level, needing to understand how mathematical abstraction might be taking place here and now, and how it might be influenced by experience; at this level, abstraction is not so much an achievement as an emergent process. Whereas at the macro-level the specific setting is inconsequential, at the micro-level it is reasonable to suppose that the structuring forces in a setting might play a key role in mathematical abstraction (Lave, 1988).

Noss and Hoyles (1996) have proposed a view of mathematical abstraction that embraces the role of the setting. They refer to a complex network of resources, some of which are internal and some of which are external (artefacts, peers, tools) and propose that meaning-making takes place by forging and re-forging connections across that network, a process they call 'webbing'. A key construct in webbing is that of 'situated abstraction'. The situated abstraction is an internal resource that emerges through webbing activity. This resource serves as a fairly general heuristic for making sense of situations that arise in a setting and is inevitably couched in the terminology and discourse of that setting. The heuristic may be conjectural in the sense that it proposes how systems and objects within the setting seem to behave, and further webbing may test that proposal. At other times, the heuristic may seem more like a conclusion or inference. Either way, the situated abstraction provides an active description, perhaps temporary, of how things get done across a setting. The webbing perspective, and its key construct of situated abstraction, in effect propose that abstraction takes place in a situation and is articulated through that situation, in contrast to the view of formal abstraction, which seeks to remove all reference to situation.

The ideas of Noss and Hoyles emerge from the observation of students who are trying to make sense of the behaviour of on-screen virtual objects through the use of carefully designed tools. The early work referred to programming in Logo, a high-level language designed to support mathematising and problem solving through a microworld, in which a turtle object can be animated to create pictures and movement. In Logo, the tools are essentially symbolic, commands and structures within the language. More recent work has drawn on iconic representations, in the form of quasi-concrete objects that represent powerful ideas in mathematics. In this respect, the role of digital technology becomes a key focus for the phenomenalisation of mathematics (Pratt, 1998).

Pratt and Noss (2002) have described the micro-evolution of knowledge that takes place when students abstract mathematical meanings when webbing with external tools and resources. This paper will first summarise their model in order to establish the theoretical framework that will underpin the subsequent illustrations of how principled design with digital technology can make mathematics phenomenal.

The micro-evolution of mathematical knowledge

Pratt and Noss's (2002) model of the micro-evolution of knowledge develops out of diSessa's Knowledge-in-Pieces (KiP) theory (1993), in which he argues that conceptual knowledge (or co-ordination classes in diSessa's terminology) emerges out of a fractured sense-making mechanism. At the outset, knowledge consists of many small pieces, referred to as phenomenological primitives (p-prims for short). An example is 'I push; it moves', though diSessa insists that p-prims are so very small that their articulation in language overstates their grain size. P-prims are typically disconnected and so are triggered independently by incoming data. To the observer, a student's response might appear inconsistent from moment to moment as the sense-making apparatus triggered is sensitive to small differences in what is attended to within the external phenomena. Learning, or tuning towards expertise, takes place as p-prims gradually become connected when they are triggered simultaneously and consistently by specific phenomena. P-prims contain cueing and reliability priorities, which change as a result of their consistency or otherwise with other p-prims and their evident post-hoc explanatory power. As the priorities change, 'successful' p-prims or collections of connected p-prims become increasingly likely to be cued in the future.

Pratt and Noss (2002) reported on students' initial naive mathematical and statistical articulations, but recognised in them potential resources for more sophisticated knowledge. By working with carefully designed digital tools, they traced the emergence of situated abstractions that captured relatively general behaviour and yet were articulated in terms of the setting being experienced. They borrowed from diSessa's KiP theory the notion that the student's initial knowledge was fractured; the situated abstractions that began to emerge seemed to reflect clusters of p-prims though nevertheless still possessing the essential p-prim causal structure in which one condition entails another (vis-à-vis 'I push; it moves'). They also observed how the students were reluctant to re-use situated abstractions recently learned; rather they would tend to draw on long-standing knowledge. Insofar as these situated abstractions were underpinned by p-prims, this observation was consistent with a low priority associated with the recent knowledge and a relatively high priority attached to the more established knowledge. Nevertheless, Pratt and Noss also observed students, who were striving to make sense of on-screen stochastic behaviour (see Scenario 4 below), drawing on recently constructed situated abstractions when feedback demonstrated that the more established ideas simply lacked explanatory power.

This observation suggests that the assertion that knowledge is situated and essentially not transferable (indeed, according to Lave, 1988, transfer simply does not exist as a construct) is consistent with the reluctance to apply situated abstractions in novel ways where the associated priorities might be low when compared to those of long-standing knowledge. At the same time, Pratt and Noss's study suggests that such knowledge does have the potential to be re-used if the activity framework supports tuning towards expertise.

As proposed by the 'Street Mathematics' research (Nunes *et al.*, 1993), the meaningfulness of the mathematics seems key. In terms of the micro-evolution of knowledge, meaningfulness across situations seems to be tied to a contextual *neighbourhood* that describes the essential conditions, purposes and features under which the situated abstraction was constructed. As will be illustrated below, many so-called reported misconceptions can be interpreted as: (i) a lack of awareness of the power of a mathematical idea to extend to other situations, reflecting a contextual neighbourhood that is currently too narrow; (ii) an over-generalisation where the limitations of the idea have not yet been recognised, indicating a contextual neighbourhood that is too broad. Evidence from the Pratt and Noss research suggests that the contextual neighbourhood can gradually extend so that, at this micro-level, decontextualisation is illusory; the mathematical knowledge represented in textbooks and university courses demonstrates the wide contextual neighbourhood that gives the knowledge wide scope and power.

Meaningfulness not only emerges out of experience, but also promotes engagement out of growing awareness of the power of the subject so that the two meanings of 'phenomenal' begin to merge. In the next section, I will illustrate the micro-evolution of mathematical knowledge through a series of short examples, and infer design principles that might facilitate not only the micro-evolution of mathematical knowledge but also engagement in the power of mathematics.

Illustrative scenarios

Five brief scenarios are presented below to illustrate aspects of making mathematics phenomenal.

Scenario 1: Using Newton's Laws before 'knowing' them

The first example revisits work that took place during my time as a school teacher in the 1980s. Newton's Laws of Motion offer a singular challenge to A Level students. Some researchers refer to the misconceptions or pre-conceptions students have for Newton's Laws (for example, Clement, 1982). For example, a student might believe that objects gradually slow down unless a force propels them forward, an Aristotelian view of motion. To support a Newtonian view, I designed physical experiments, such as sliding objects down slopes, but found them to be unhelpful; it seemed that, because friction was ever present in these material situations, there was a need to create an artificial world in which any object would move only according to Newtonian forces explicitly created by the students.

The software, Newton, was built in Logo with the explicit aim of situating students in such an artificial microworld (Pratt, 1988). Newton was built on top of Logo so that the students would be able to develop extended projects in the spirit of Harel and Papert's Constructionism (1991). One example of a sub-task within Newton is given below. The student is challenged to make an object slide down a slope.

In Figure 1, the student has applied a weight force vertically down the screen and a friction force against the direction of motion down the slope. These are two forces that students at this age typically already know about. However, when the system is set in motion, the two forces combine in such a way that the object accelerates parabolically into the slope, rather than down it. Only later, when the student adds a normal reaction force (Figure 2), might the object slide down the plane.

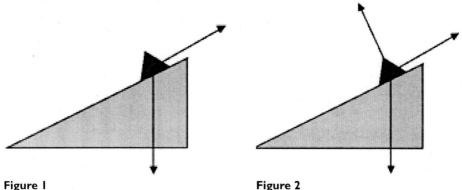

Figure 1   **Figure 2**

In this way, the student might recognise the need for a normal reaction force if objects are to behave consistently with everyday observation. The normal reaction force lives in the student's web of reasons. The material world supports an Aristotelian view of motion since objects slow down naturally through the action of hidden friction and only maintain speed, accelerate, or slow suddenly through the action of external forces (such as braking). The reason for a normal reaction force remains obscure. In Newton, all forces have equal status;

weights, frictions, reaction and tractive forces all have to be programmed into the system by the student. In this virtual world, the need for a force to bring about a change in velocity and the lack of need for a force if velocity is merely to be maintained becomes apparent.

This example illustrates the Constructionist idea that using can happen before knowing (Hoyles and Noss, 1987). Here, the students operate within a world in which Newton's Laws apply – but not automatically, as in the everyday world. In this artificial world, the students have to use Newton's Laws to create motion even though their knowledge of these laws is only emergent. Papert (1996) describes the Power Principle, in which he asserts that, conventionally, mathematics education inverts the normal way in which people learn. In most situations, he argues, people learn about a tool by using that tool. In mathematics, the normal trajectory is inverted insofar as people are presented with procedures for calculating, drawing and measuring without having the opportunity to use the mathematics for a meaningful purpose. Papert argues that digital technology offers the opportunity to re-invert that inversion since it is possible to create quasi-concrete on-screen versions of the mathematics that can be used during the creation of virtual products. The Newton task above offers a clear example of the Power Principle in operation.

Scenario 2: The utility of graphing and algebraic notation

Gaining knowledge about graphs in school curricula typically involves learning how to draw many different representations, such as bar charts, pie charts, line graphs, scatterplots and histograms. Each has its own set of conventions to be remembered and each presents challenging cognitive demands, such as scaling. Much research has shown how difficult children find it to learn these skills (Padilla *et al.*, 1986; Swatton and Taylor, 1994). Worse still, the effort needed to learn how to represent data dominates teaching and learning to the extent that little emphasis is given to the interpretation of graphs, which many might feel is a key understanding. The Swatton and Taylor research has shown that a very low percentage of secondary school-age children successfully interpret graphs.

The example below illustrates not only the use of knowledge even as it is emerging (as above) but also how graphing and algebra can be understood as synergetic productivity tools towards a defined goal. In the classic MaxBox investigation, students are challenged to find the maximum capacity open box that can be made from a piece of A4 paper by cutting equal squares from each corner. What size square creates the largest volume box (see Figure 3)?

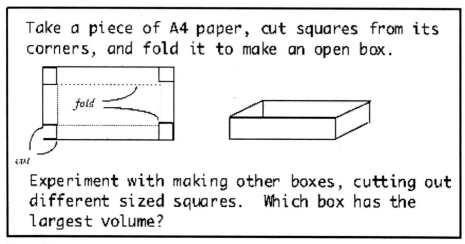

Take a piece of A4 paper, cut squares from its corners, and fold it to make an open box.

Experiment with making other boxes, cutting out different sized squares. Which box has the largest volume?

Figure 3

An active approach is to require the students physically to make the boxes and measure the dimensions of the box. These measurements are then entered into a spreadsheet, which automatically calculates the volume of the box. Figure 4 shows one student's graph when only four boxes had been made and measured. Ainley (1996) reported how this 11-year-old, after making several boxes out of A4 paper, began simply to enter box dimensions directly into the spreadsheet. The student was evidently mentally calculating the length and width of the boxes. The researcher intervened to suggest that, if he was doing a mental calculation, it should be possible to 'teach' the rule to the spreadsheet. Since he was already familiar with spreadsheets, he knew that if he were able to enter a formula (below, more detail is given on how difficult this was) and fill the formula down, he would be able to create instantly many different results, each with its calculated volume. Figure 5 depicts a graph that included some measured data alongside some data that had been generated from a formula.

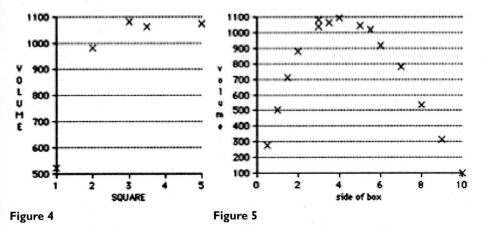

Figure 4   **Figure 5**

Creating the formula was a non-trivial step. There are many forms that the mental calculation might take. Here is one possibility: 'Double the size of the square, 5, to get 10. What do I need to add on to 10 to reach 21, the width of the paper? 11, so the width of the box is 11cm.' The spreadsheet requires a formula such as: '= 21 – 2 * B1', where the size of the square is in cell B1. The translation task from the mental formulation to the formal algebraic expression is challenging. Nevertheless, some students in the research succeeded. One reason was that the students were able to try out their ideas and benefit from feedback. Often the spreadsheet fed back an error message because the algebra was not properly formulated or it did not generate the known correct value. A second reason was that the students were familiar with the pay-off for succeeding. They understood that, once the formula had been entered correctly, many results could be generated very quickly by filling the formula down the columns of the spreadsheet. The power of filling down provided the incentive to persist in trying to teach the formula to the spreadsheet in its correct formulation.

In fact, the power of filling was sometimes further exploited. Some students filled the formula down many rows of the spreadsheet. In Figure 6, the volumes of the boxes become negative once the side of the square cut out exceeds half the width of the paper and then become positive again once the side of the square also exceeds half the length of the paper.

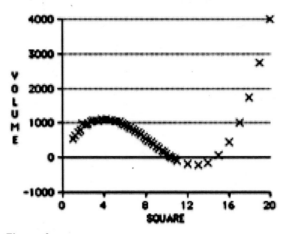

Figure 6

In this approach to MaxBox, the student might learn that both graphing and algebra have utility. The graph, usually seen as a presentational tool when the emphasis is on how it is drawn, might instead be regarded as a powerful analytical tool where the emphasis is on interpretation within an experiment or investigation. Similarly, algebra, so often seen as meaningless, can be experienced as a tool for communicating with a machine to 'get the job done'. Using before knowing and generating utility are common themes throughout these five scenarios. In the third example below, the focus is on linking utility to purpose.

Scenario 3: Purposeful geometric construction

Pratt and Ainley (1997) reported on their early work with dynamic geometry software working with primary school-age children. Their aim had been to exploit the newly available (as it was then) power of Cabri Geometry to explore the construction of figures. The challenge lay in the fact that such young children possessed very little geometric knowledge and yet, following a Constructionist approach, they sought tasks that would engage these children in such a way that they would appreciate the power of geometric construction.

Other researchers (Healy and Hoyles, 2001) had reported the notion of 'messing up'. The properties of a figure that was simply drawn in Cabri Geometry would not remain invariant when the figure was dragged. To avoid the shape becoming messed up, it must be constructed using its properties. 'Messing up' seemed to offer a promising direction. One boy, Bernard (pseudonym), had drawn a wonderfully detailed soccer pitch (Figure 7).

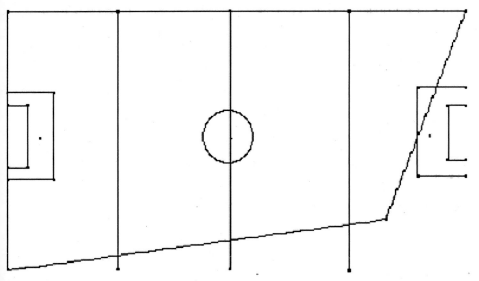

Figure 7

Pratt approached Bernard with the pedagogic construct of messing up in mind and proposed to Bernard that, if he were to pick up one corner of his soccer pitch, the rectangular pitch would lose its shape. Bernard's response was memorable. Bernard said, 'But, Dave, you wouldn't do that, would you?' The light-hearted remark does perhaps reflect the good relationship that the researchers had with these children, but it also spoke about something more profound. Though powerful, messing up retained an element of contrivance. Bernard was happy with his drawn rectangular soccer pitch. There was no need for it to be constructed. Worse still, construction would have transformed an interesting project into one that was much more challenging, but for no reason that was evident to Bernard. The children in this class produced many such carefully drawn pictures for the sheer fun of it, but they did not see any need for geometric construction.

After several months of failing to find ways of exploiting the constructional power of Cabri Geometry, Pratt and Ainley finally designed some tasks that seemed to provide a sense of how construction might be powerful. One such task drew on the fact that these children, aged 10, would regularly meet with younger reading partners, aged 6, to help them with their reading.

The 10-year-olds were challenged to design a drawing kit for their reading partners. The aim was to create a set of shapes that could be the building bricks for a drawing, which their reading partners would put together. There was a self-evident need for the shapes to be constructed, since the shapes would lose their essential features, as soon as they were dragged into position by their reading partners. Within this context it made sense to provide some initial starting points, such as how to construct an equilateral triangle. The children worked for extended periods to create elements of their drawing kit. Figure 8 shows a wheel and a house shape, both perfectly constructed so that the properties would remain invariant when dragged by the reading partners.

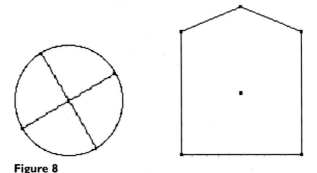

Figure 8

Figure 9 shows one child's final report after the task was completed.

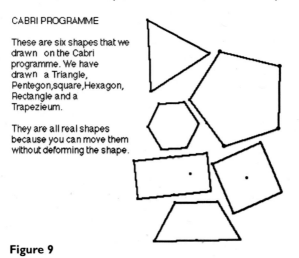

CABRI PROGRAMME

These are six shapes that we drawn on the Cabri programme. We have drawn a Triangle, Pentegon,square,Hexagon, Rectangle and a Trapezieum.

They are all real shapes because you can move them without deforming the shape.

Figure 9

The drawing kit task illustrates how children can gain a sense of the power of a mathematical idea, in this case geometric construction, when engaged in purposeful activity. The story also indicates that designing tasks that potentially connect purpose with utility is far from trivial; in fact, this design skill, which seeks to offer child-friendly inferential reasons for the mathematical notion, will need to be emphasised in the effort to make mathematics more phenomenal.

Scenario 4: Controlling and representing the behaviour of a die

The above three examples illustrate how making mathematics phenomenal involves transforming mathematical concepts into a form that allows students to engage directly with them, and that virtual environments such as microworlds, spreadsheets and dynamic geometry can support such an endeavour. Considerable emphasis is also placed in these examples on task design, in such a way that the mathematics is experienced through purposeful activity that engenders a sense of the power or utility of the concept. The ChanceMaker study (Pratt, 1998) continues to illustrate this theme, but identifies a particular design construct that supports designing for abstraction (Pratt and Noss, 2010), a design construct that places control in the hands of the student in such a way that the control becomes a representation of the concept.

The ChanceMaker study created gadgets, digital simulations of everyday devices that generate random outcomes. The students were challenged to decide which of the gadgets were 'working properly'. One such case is the standard six-sided die. Students, aged 11, were able to play with the computer die to generate results much like throwing a standard die by pulling on the strength control as in Figure 10. In fact, this gadget was intentionally 'broken' in that it was programmed to generate more sixes. Later, they were further challenged to 'mend' the die to make it 'work properly' using the tools revealed when the die was opened up. In Figure 11, the student has already thrown the die 14 times. The set of results is listed and can be scrutinised by scrolling down. A pie chart graphically displays the results of those 14 throws. The research demonstrated how students would typically decide at this point that the die was generating too many sixes and mend the gadget by editing the workings box to read 'choose-from [1 2 3 4 5 6]'.

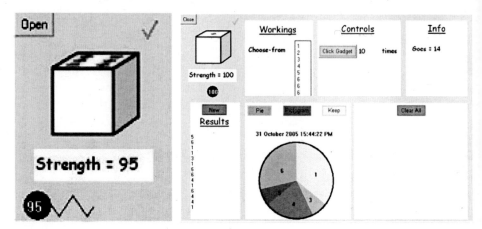

Figure 10   **Figure 11**

It might be thought that the problem was thus solved, but the research revealed how the students did not realise this. When they threw the die to test their apparent solution, it would not generate the uniform pie chart they expected. If the pie chart showed too few 3s (for example), they might remove the 3 from the workings box and try again. This time there would be no 3s and perhaps too few 1s (say) as well. So they might then reinsert the 3 and add an additional 1. This process would continue until, either out of exasperation or by good fortune, they would hit upon the idea of throwing the die more times. Using the 'repeat' control, the students could throw the die as many times as they liked but, until that point, such an action had not been thought to be necessary. Once they tried this, the students began to deduce that 'the more times they throw the die, the more even is its pie chart'. Later, some students recognised the pivotal role of the workings box and that, provided the die was thrown a lot of times, the pie chart would reflect the distribution in the workings box, whatever it might be.

In ChanceMaker, the students were given the workings box so that they were able to control the configuration of the die (and the other gadgets) and so mend it. The students were able to experience randomness and began to discern differences between short-term and long-term behaviour. Eventually some of the students were able to inspect any given workings box and predict the long-term behaviour of the corresponding die without conducting the experiment. In this sense, the workings box had become a representation of the mathematical notion of distribution. The activity in ChanceMaker illustrates perfectly the critical role of experience in providing opportunity to test out personal conjectures, to refute certain ideas and develop new ones. The task, to identify and then mend broken gadgets, generated purposeful activity that led to a sense of the utility of the workings box to predict behaviour. The workings box ultimately fused initial control over activity with representation of predicted behaviour. The design objective could be stated as seeking to blur control and representation to create what Noss and Hoyles (1996) have referred to as *auto-expressive* tools. The blurring of control and representation in effect acknowledges the relationship between reasons ('the workings box provides me with a means to explore my ideas') and representations ('the workings box states the expected behaviour of the die') in the mind, as proposed by the inferentialist philosophy.

Scenario 5: Expressing mathematics in socially complex situations

Another key aspect of the above four examples has been that the environment encourages the students to express their mathematical ideas. In Newton, the students were able to create motion by applying forces. Beyond this, they could use the broader Logo language to develop larger projects, such as simulating the elliptical motion of planets. When using a spreadsheet to create scattergraphs, the children expressed their ideas for the formula that connected the side of the square cut out to the length and width of the open box. In the drawing kit task, the children created constructed figures that could be used by their reading partners as elements of a picture. In ChanceMaker, the workings box was used to express how the die gadget should behave.

The final scenario elaborates a situation that is focused on a less well-defined concept than any of the above. Mathematics as it is applied in everyday contexts typically manifests itself in models in which decision making requires consideration of elements that are not so easily mathematised. Yet, the social context for the application of such mathematics can offer a sense of the power and limitations of the discipline that cannot be found in its more conventional teaching. Two brief illustrations will suffice.

As part of the Bowland project (www.bowlandmaths.org.uk/casestudies.htm), one case study was to plan a highway link around a village. The students needed to consider which route the by-pass should take. Figure 12 shows the map that was given to the students and two possible routes under consideration. These two routes had been created and can be measured using the digital tools.

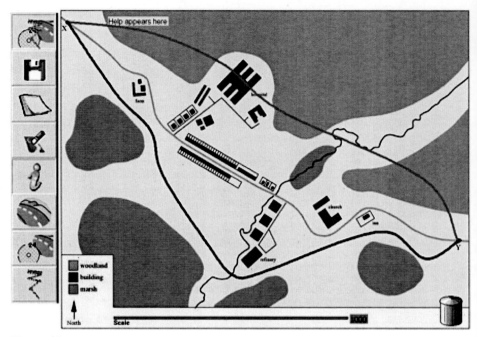

Figure 12

The upper route is far shorter than the lower route and so, when the students calculate the cost of building this route, it will be considerably lower than the cost of the lower route. The social cost of the upper route may, however, be thought to be much higher since it would involve deforestation and the destruction of a hospital. As well as considering costs and ethical issues, the students would need to check safety information. For example, the curvature, which can be measured using another tool in the software, of the final bend in the lower route may be too acute and so break regulations. Perhaps the planning meeting that the class would hold at the end of the exploration would reject both of these routes and agree a compromise solution.

The second illustration of the use of mathematics in social contexts focuses on risk-based decision making. In a recent project funded by the Wellcome Foundation, secondary school mathematics and science teachers' understanding, including pedagogic knowledge, of risk was explored. The project was a starting point for a longer-term enterprise to inform the teaching and learning of risk, which has recently entered the mathematics and science curricula.

During the project, a microworld called Deborah's Dilemma was designed in which the teachers were required to consider the plight of a fictitious young woman, Deborah. Deborah suffered from a back condition for which she could decide to have an operation. The teachers were given information about the working and social life of Deborah. They were also informed about the condition itself, the operation and the possible consequences. Much of this data was inconsistent. For example, Deborah had consulted three different doctors and she had also done some personal research on the internet. The results were sometimes contradictory and sometimes vague, rather like everyday decision making.

The teachers were asked to create models of what might happen if Deborah were to choose to have the operation. In Figure 13, the teachers have entered an overall success rate of 70 per cent and chosen to focus on three side-effects of varying degrees of seriousness, each with its own estimated likelihood. The teachers have decided on these values according to their interpretation of the information given. The patchwork chart shows what might happen in 1,000 of Deborah's possible futures. In this set of outcomes, no paralysis occurred, though there is an instance of superbug infection and several cases of nerve damage. In most cases, the operation was successful.

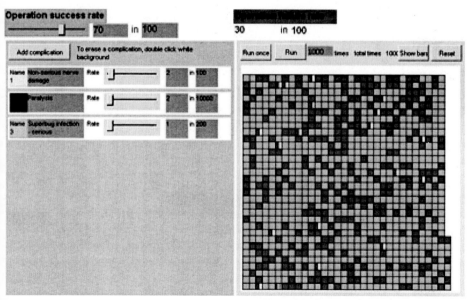

Figure 13

To consider further Deborah's plight, the teachers also needed to consider what might happen if Deborah did not choose to have the operation. In Figure 14, the teachers have modelled Deborah's life using three activities.

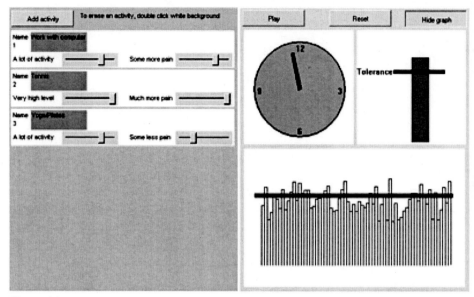

Figure 14

Each of these activities might take place frequently or rarely and each creates additional pain or relieves some pain. The teachers decide on these settings according to their interpretation of the information they have read. The bar in the top right indicates the level of pain that Deborah is experiencing hour to hour as a result of the model being run. The teachers can judge whether this level of pain is tolerable or not.

The intention in Deborah's Dilemma is to probe the teachers' knowledge about risk by observing how they create their models. Further developments might seek in a similar way to sensitise students to the issues in making judgements about risk. In particular, risk-based decision making needs to consider impact and likelihood of hazards, but exactly how these factors might be co-ordinated depends critically on subjective judgements involving the values of the decision maker (Pratt *et al.*, 2011).

In the Highway Link and Deborah's Dilemma, the students began to map out the inferentialist domain of the territory of mathematics. These examples emphasise that an aspect of making mathematics phenomenal is to experience the power and scope of mathematics in socially oriented decision making.

Abstraction and the power to engage

In this final section, I wish to re-examine the notion of making mathematics phenomenal in the light of the above five scenarios. The project requires that the mathematical ideas are phenomenalised as on-screen tools in such a way that situated abstractions of the concepts are constructed. The design of the tools is extremely important. We have seen the benefits when the tools are expressive and connect control and representation. The task design is equally crucial. The examples demonstrate the need for tasks, which will be seen as purposeful by the students. In these scenarios, purpose is generated because the task involves a problem that piques curiosity, exercises creativity or interfaces with social concerns (Ainley *et al.*, 2006). Purpose is, however, insufficient. The mathematics teacher has an agenda to observe and this agenda requires introducing students to powerful mathematical ideas.

In the above examples, mathematics is experienced as something with utility. Utility is a difficult word since it might be taken to infer pragmatic usefulness such as when compound interest might be taught because one day it will be useful to the students when they have to deal with bank accounts, mortgages and investments. Utility refers to the power of a mathematical idea to get things done that are meaningful and important to the student in that moment. For some students, utility might even emerge in pure mathematics. Imagine a microworld focused on symmetry and permutations, and the excitement that could be triggered for some students when the same group language might be used to create combinations of either symmetries or permutations.

Utility is an aspect of mathematical understanding that has been largely forgotten. When Skemp (1976) discussed instrumental understanding, he referred to the sort of routine and procedural knowledge that might, for example, underpin the execution of certain algorithms such as subtracting by decomposition. When he referred to relational understanding, the focus was on the appreciation of how the mathematics worked and connections between apparently different aspects of the discipline. For example, decomposition might be understood through place value. Neither the instrumental nor the relational components properly capture utility-based understanding, which focuses on when mathematics might be powerful.

By making mathematics phenomenal, the claim is that it is possible to engender utility-based understanding. In the context of the five scenarios above, the students make sense of the behaviour of on-screen objects through carefully designed tools. There is committed purpose in that sense-making activity, a need to find an explanation. In inferentialist language, the students initially find their reasons for engagement in the nature of the task, but this develops into an appreciation of the power of the mathematics itself to get the job done. In this sense, the locus of the reasons for engagement in the task merges with reasons for engagement with the mathematics. Their expressions of general behaviour, referred to above as situated abstraction, are sometimes wrong or only half true from the perspective of an informed outside observer and reflect the gradual cohering of fractured knowledge, as in diSessa's framework. Let us further review utility by revisiting each of the five scenarios.

In Newton, the creative application of forces in a problem-solving or project context offered purposeful activity that could lead to the construction of situated abstractions for Newton's Laws, such as 'the normal reaction force makes the turtle stay on the slope'. The power or utility of Newton's Laws lies in how they get that job done; it keeps the turtle on the slope. This is not of course the whole story. Situated abstractions are only ever a partial truth.

In the MaxBox scenario, the clear challenge of finding the maximum volume box, set initially in a practical exercise, created a purposeful setting in which students could construct utility for algebra. The spreadsheet formula '=21 – 2 * B1' can be filled down to generate many boxes enabling a graph to be generated from which the maximum can be read. A situated abstraction might be 'the spreadsheet formula generates lots of results'.

In the drawing kit task, the children are excited by the idea of creating a tool for their reading partners, but that task is carefully linked to the utility of geometric construction since the job can only get done through that approach. The children appeared to construct situated abstractions such as, 'the constructed wheel does not get messed up when my reading partner uses it'.

In ChanceMaker, the purposeful activity is generated by the challenge of mending the gadgets and this can lead to situated abstractions such as 'the more times I throw the die, the more uniform is the pie chart' and 'the pie chart matches the workings box, provided I throw the die lots of times'. These situated abstractions express utilities for repetition over the long term and for the notion of distribution.

In the Highway Link and Deborah's Dilemma, there is a sense of the utility of mathematics in decision making. In the former, there might be a situated abstraction 'longer routes cost more but they might be better because they avoid knocking down the hospital'. In the latter, a situated abstraction might be 'I need to decide, so as to balance the impact of hazards with their likelihoods'.

In each scenario, key mathematical ideas are phenomenalised in the sense that the tools and tasks offer direct experience of the mathematics. The utility emerged out of a sense of purpose; it is such power to engage that could create a widely felt sense of the extraordinariness of mathematics. Making mathematics phenomenal involves respecting students' reasons for engagement, recognising that human knowledge is inferential. In contrast, typical mathematics curricula set out syllabi that place huge emphasis on lists of graphical and numerical representations.

Consider, for example, the handling data attainment target in the current National Curriculum. This is replete with various graphs such as bar charts, line graphs, scatterplots and histograms and measures such as mean, mode and median, interquartile range and standard deviation, to name just a few. Little emphasis is given to the data handling cycle and statistical inference that might better approximate what it means to do statistics and map out the territory by establishing the power and scope of statistical ideas to elaborate meaningful questions. As a result, our students can become proficient in drawing graphs and making calculations without ever knowing what statistics is fundamentally about. A statistics curriculum that paid proper attention to the discipline as a human enterprise might be founded on inferentialist philosophy and developed upon Constructionist design principles.

Inferentialism offers a powerful philosophical account of how the Constructionist emphasis on the creation of public products might offer purposeful tasks that generate utility for mathematical ideas by placing priority on reasons for engagement. Through the connection of purpose and utility, perhaps mathematics might be made phenomenal.

References

Ainley, J. (1996) 'Purposeful contexts for formal notation in a spreadsheet environment'. *Journal of Mathematical Behavior*, 15(4), 405–22.

Ainley, J., Pratt, D. and Hansen, A. (2006) 'Connecting engagement and focus in pedagogic task design'. *British Educational Research Journal*, 32(1), 23–38.

Brandom, R. (2002) 'Overcoming a dualism of concepts and causes: A unifying thread in "empiricism and the philosophy of mind"'. In R.M. Gale (ed.), *Blackwell Guide to Metaphysics* (pp. 263–81). Oxford: Blackwell.

Brown, M., Brown, P. and Bibby, T. (2008) '"I would rather die": Reasons given by 16-year-olds for not continuing their study of mathematics'. *Research in Mathematics Education*, 10(1), 3–18.

Clement, J. (1982) 'Students' preconceptions in introductory mechanics'. *American Journal of Physics*, 50, 66–71.

Confrey, J. and Costa, S. (1996) 'A critique of the selection of "mathematical objects" as a central metaphor for Advanced Mathematical Thinking'. *International Journal of Computers for Mathematical Learning*, 1(2), 139–68.

diSessa, A. (1993) 'Towards an epistemology of physics'. *Cognition and Instruction*, 10, 105–226.

Dubinsky, E. (1991) 'Reflective abstraction in advanced mathematical thinking'. In D. Tall (ed.), *Advanced Mathematical Thinking* (pp. 95–123). Dordrecht: Kluwer.

Gray, E.M. and Tall, D.O. (1994) 'Duality, ambiguity and flexibility: A proceptual view of simple arithmetic'. *Journal for Research in Mathematics Education*, 26, 115–41.

Harel, I. and Papert, S. (1991) *Constructionism*. Norwood, New Jersey: Ablex.

Healy, L. and Hoyles, C. (2001) 'Software tools for geometric problem solving: Potentials and pitfalls'. *International Journal for Computers and Mathematical Learning*, 6(3), 235–56.

Hoyles, C. and Noss, R. (1987) 'Children working in a structured Logo environment: From doing to understanding'. *Recherches en Didactiques des Mathematiques*, 8(12), 131–74.

Lave, J. (1988) *Cognition in Practice*. Cambridge: Cambridge University Press.

Noss, R. and Hoyles, C. (1996) *Windows on mathematical meanings: Learning cultures and computers*. London: Kluwer.

Nunes, T., Schliemann, A.D. and Carraher, D.W. (1993) *Street Mathematics and School Mathematics*. Cambridge: Cambridge University Press.

Osborne, J., Black, P. and Boaler, J. (1997) *Attitudes to Science, Mathematics and Technology: A review of research*. London: King's College, University of London.

Padilla, M.J., McKenzie, D.L. and Shaw, E.L. (1986) 'An examination of the line graphing ability of students in grades seven through twelve'. *School Science and Mathematics*, 86, 20–6.

Papert, S. (1996) 'An exploration in the space of mathematics educations'. *International Journal of Computers for Mathematical Learning*, 1(1), 95–123.

Pratt, D. (1988) 'Taking a dive with Newton'. *Micromath*, 4(1), 33–5.

Pratt, D. (1998) 'Meanings *in* and meanings *for* a domain of stochastic abstraction'. Unpublished PhD thesis, University of London.

Pratt, D. and Ainley, J. (1997) 'The construction of meanings for geometric construction: Two contrasting cases'. *International Journal of Computers for Mathematical Learning*, 1(3), 293–322.

Pratt, D. and Noss, R. (2002) 'The micro-evolution of mathematical knowledge: The case of randomness'. *Journal of the Learning Sciences*, 11(4), 453–88.

Pratt, D. and Noss, R. (2010) 'Designing for mathematical abstraction'. *International Journal of Computers for Mathematical Learning*, 15(2), 81–97.

Pratt, D., Ainley, J., Kent, P., Levinson, R., Yogui, C. and Kapadia, R. (2011) 'Informal inferential reasoning as a contextualised risk-based enterprise'. *Mathematical Thinking and Learning*, 13(4), 322–45.

Sfard, A. (1991) 'On the dual nature of mathematical conceptions: Reflections on process and objects as different sides of the same coin'. *Educational Studies in Mathematics*, 22, 1–36.

Sfard, A. (1994) 'Reification as the birth of metaphor'. *For the Learning of Mathematics*, 14(1), 44–55.

Skemp, R.R. (1976) 'Relational understanding and instrumental understanding'. *Mathematics Teaching*, 77, 20–6.

Swatton, P. and Taylor, R.M. (1994) 'Pupil performance in graphical tasks and its relationship to the ability to handle variables'. *British Educational Research Journal*, 20(2), 227–43.